Iconic
LONDON

Simon Hadleigh-Sparks

NH
NEW HOLLAND

Dedicated to London –
For My Mum, Em & Moll x

INTRODUCTION

"Photography starts with the push of the shutter button.
It doesn't end there, it never has, it never will."

Not another book about London? How many do we need! This beautiful book, however, is a photographic moment of the here and now in London, and you are invited in to share in that moment.

There are literally thousands of pictures taken of the Royal Albert Hall, Trafalgar Square and Buckingham Palace but how many showcase a particular feature, an angle, an effect … something unusual and unique, whilst staying true to the original image? Did you know there was a ship on top of Liberty's? Or three naked golden ladies leaping off the roof in Piccadilly?

This lavishly produced book will help you see London as you've never seen it before, renewing the relationship for those that call it home or perhaps beginning one for those who have yet to discover what this vibrant, noisy, multicultural city has to offer.

London is an ever-changing city, blink and one building disappears and another appears – bigger, taller and shinier. In ten years from now, how many photos would be the same? This is London today, as the city is rarely seen.

Enjoy this book from the comfort of your sofa, on the train journey home from work or on the plane back to wherever you may call home, and it is easy to imagine you are actually in one of the most iconic cities in the world … **Iconic London**.

Simon Hadleigh-Sparks is an award-winning London-based photographer who draws his inspiration from the city around him. He utilises a mixture of styles, but currently leans heavily towards urban/city photography and modern architecture, sometimes adding a twist, an angle or a feature. It is in post-production where his photos come alive as he experiments with different techniques to create eye-catching images. This is the first of a planned three-book series with New Holland Publishers.

ArcelorMittal Orbit Olympic Park at Night

8

Attack of the Monsters – Driving Down
London Fenchurch Street

Batman To Gotham – The New Adelphi –
Art Deco 1930s London

BBC Broadcasting House –Portland Place.

Elizabeth Tower — Big Ben, and a London Bus.

11

Blackfriars Bridge and the City Skyline

12

Broadgate Tower – 201 Bishopsgate

14

Broadgate Tower – Skyfall James Bond Tower

15

The BT Tower (Post Office Tower) Fitzrovia

A Royal Swan outside of Buckingham Palace

Buckingham Palace

18

20

Business Or Religion? A New World Order – The Gherkin with St Andrew Undershaft

Bustle At Borough Market Southwark

Can You Do The Cube – Fleet Place Office Building

The Financial Giants Running Out Of Sky — Canary Wharf

*Canary Wharf Inner Dock Milwall
(Pan Peninsula East Tower)*

Night Reflections – Canary Wharf North Dock

Canary Wharf Skyline Reflected, 2015.

London's Busiest Station – Canary Wharf Underground Station

Famous For Its Shopping —Carnaby Street

Central Saint Giles Buildings

31

Centrepoint – The Centre of London

Changing of The Guard – Horse Guards Parade

33

Chinese New Year – Gerrard Street, China Town

34

The Shard and Surrounding City Hall Area – Southwark, South Bank,
River Thame

The Queen's Walk, City Hall

Eye In The Summer Blue Sky — The London Eye

Coca Cola Takes Over The London Eye 2015 –
The London Eye

Dream World –The London Eye

A Carousel and The London Eye – Southbank

London Bus Lightspeed

Blue Christmas – The London Eye

Winter Morning – The London Eye

44

London Green Eye

Quiet Winter Morning – Covent Garden

Quiet Winter Morning – Covent Garden

49

'Don't be sad its over be glad and smile we were there' – London 2012 Olympic Stadium

Olympic Stadium – 2013
Anniversary

Dawn Of A New Era – Olympic
Stadium, London 2012

Elizabeth Tower & Big Ben

*Entrance To St Paul's
Cathedral West Door*

Financial Revolution – Canary Wharf

Curve Your World – Florin Court, Smithfield

Not Just Urban City But Many Green Spaces & Parks – Syon Park

63

Greenwich O2 Arena (The Millenium Dome)

Under The Millennium Dome – The Greenwich O2
Arena

Greenwich Royal Naval College & Canary Wharf

The Third Tallest Building in Greater London – Heron Tower, 110 Bishopgate

69

Hammersmith Suspension Bridge at Night

Horse Guards Parade Whitehall

Horses of Helios – Piccadilly Circus

Hotel Russell – Russell Square Bloomsbury

Houses of Parliament & Big Ben – River Thames

Houses of Parliament & Westminster Bridge

Big Ben – Neon Westminster

Night On The Town – Big Ben

Ice Skating At Somerset House, The Strand

80

In A Spin At The Southbank Christmas – Southbank

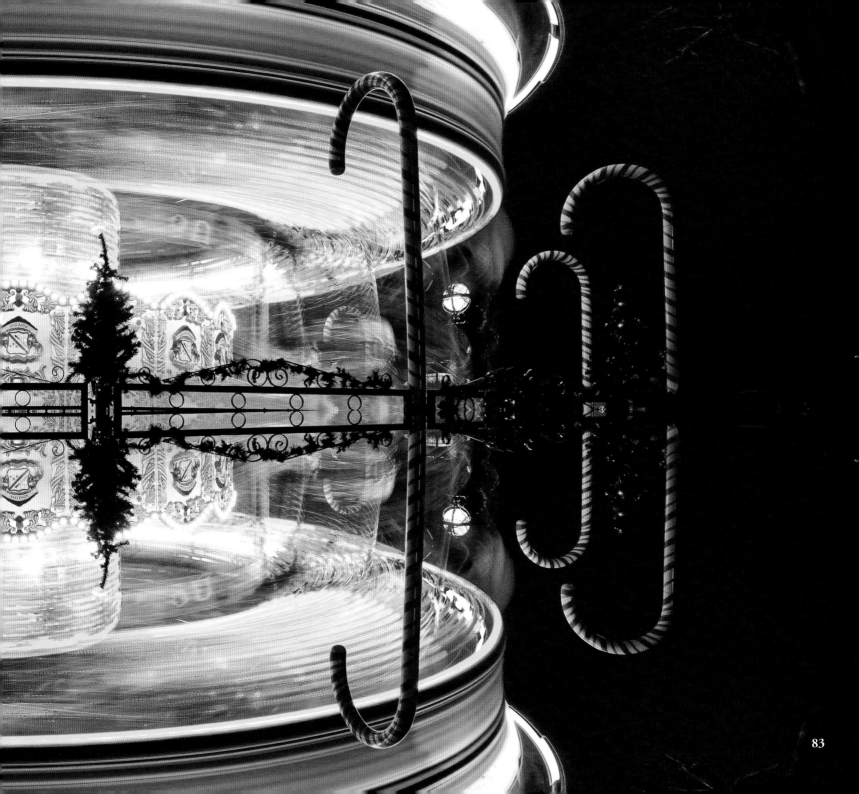

Kew Gardens – Davies Alpine House

Kew Gardens – The Palm House

85

Roof Architecture – King's Cross Station

Leadenhall Covered Market At
Christmas – Gracechurch Street

Liberty Department Store (Note the ship on the roof)– Regents Street

Living In The Shadows Of Giants, Central London

London City Love – 99 Bishopsgate

'London City Eye' – Park Tower Casino

London City Life – Westminster

Eros Statue & The Piccadilly Circus Big Screen

London In Motion –
Piccadilly Circus

Piccadilly Circus Blended

*Cubism – London Rubik's Cube
Building by London Bridge*

London Skyline & Thames East

London Skyline & Thames West

London Skyline Sunshine & Cloud

Well They Had To Appear – *London's Red Telephone Boxes*

Look Across Our City – Olympic Park & Canary Wharf

Lost In London – Millenium Bridge & St Paul's

The Millenium Bridge & Tate Modern Art Gallery

Marble Arch – Park Lane, Oxford Street

111

Metropolis (Future Today) – London City Office Life
Walkie Talkie, Willis & Lloyds Buildings

Mid Winter – Canary Wharf & River Thames

Blackfriars Bridge & The City

Moonlight Over Albert Bridge Chelsea

National Gallery – Trafalger Square Christmas

No 1 Poultry, London City Architecture – Queen Victoria Street

121

Not A Cloud In The Sky – The Walkie Talkie

art/theatre/music
dance/film/education
conferences/library
restaurants/bars

barbican

FOODHALL

Oasis In The City – The Barbican Performing Arts Centre

London Stock Exchange – Paternoster Square

Mind The Gap – The Tube, London Underground

126

Christmas – Regent Street

127

Retro Vision of the Future – 140 London Wall

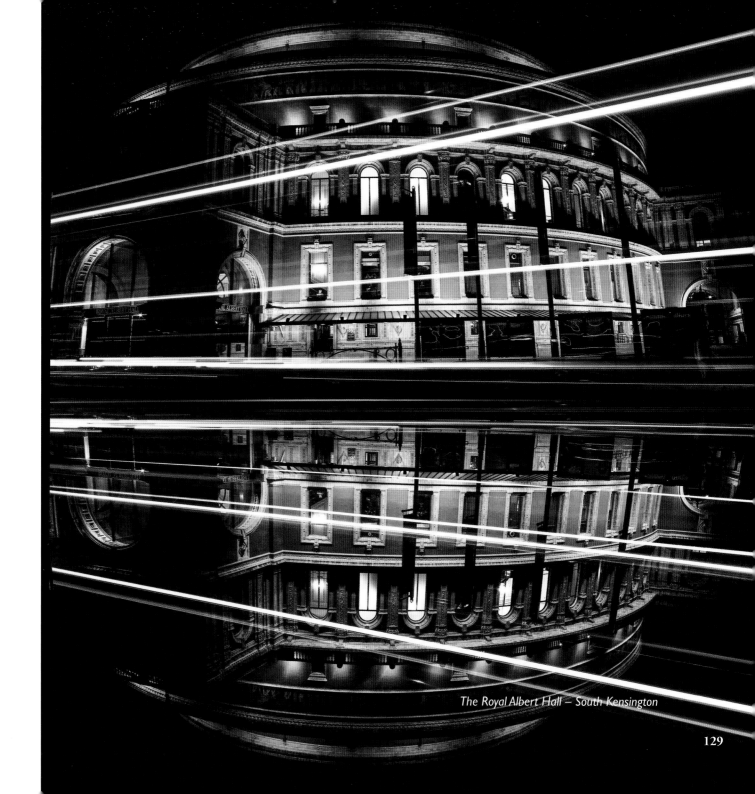

The Royal Albert Hall – South Kensington

DEFEND·THE·CHILDREN·OF·THE· POOR·&·PVNISH·THE·WRONGDOER·

130

The Old Bailey – Central Criminal Court

Royal National Theatre – Southbank

*Shakespeare's The Globe Theatre –
Bankside*

Shoreditch Street Art

133

Relflections – St Paul's Cathedral

Harrow On The Hill – Skyline London City From Afar

135

Christmas in Sloane Square

The Iconic Buildings – London City

137

Southwark Underground Tube Station

138

Spiral Staircase – The Chapel of the Old Royal Naval College

St Bride's Church – Spire Fleet Street

St George Wharf Reflections – Lambeth

Mirror Mirror – St Paul's Cathedral

The City Reflects — St Paul's Cathedral

Most Photographed Building In London –
St Paul's Cathedral

Surprise Party – St Paul's Cathedral

Fly By – St Paul's Cathedral London

Sunset Behind The Houses of Parliament Palace of Westminster

Sunset On The Towers

Sunset – The Shard & HMS Belfast

151

The Great Conservatory by Night — Syon House

The Great Conservatory Winter – Syon House

Syon House in Winter

The Batman Building – #7
More London

The Batman Building – London Estates

The Thames Barrier – Downstream River Defence

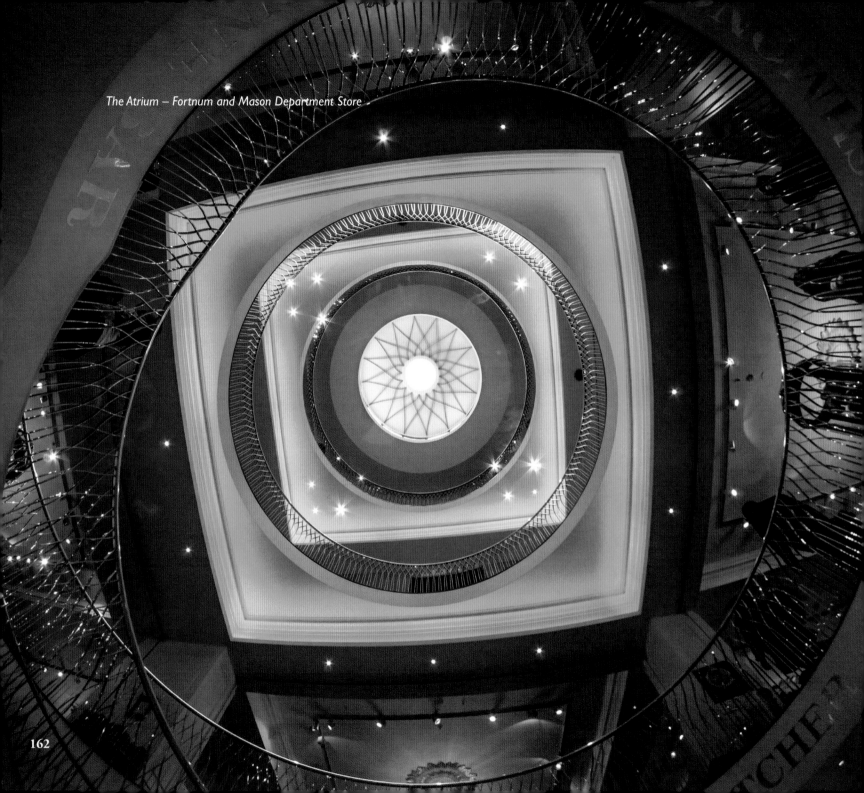

The Atrium – Fortnum and Mason Department Store

The Great Web – British Museum Bloomsbury

The London Palladium – West End Theatre

The New Adelphi – Art Deco 1930's London

ADELPHI

TO 10 JOHN STREET

The Newest Form of Public Transport – Boris Bikes

The Olympic Rings Under the Roof of St Pancras Station

168

The Savoy Hotel On The Strand

The Scoop – Outdoor Amphitheatre

The View – The Shard (On Southwark Bridge)

The Three Graces of
Piccadilly Criterion Building

171

The Thames At Low Tide

The Tower – St George Wharf Tower

The Underground Symbol, found all around London

OXFORD
CIRCUS W1
CITY OF WESTMINSTER

UNDERGROUND

↑ Bond Street ⊖ 🚶
5 minute walk along Oxford Street

← Piccadilly Circus ⊖ 🚶
9 minute walk along Regent Street

Through The Eye – Royal Festival Hall

176

Through The Looking Glass – Lloyds & Willis Building

Towards The Tower – London Riverside

Fill The Sky — Tower 42

Tower Bridge & The Shard

Night Light Trails — Tower Bridge

Tower of London & Tower Bridge Skyline

Love London – Trafalgar Square & Nelsons Column

Trafalgar Square at Night

Tunnel Vision – Greenwich Foot Tunnel

Unoriginal Icons – St Paul's Cathedral, The West Front

Henry Cole Wing — Victoria & Albert Museum

191

We're Not In Kansas Anymore – The Gherkin & The Cheesegrater

Westminster Abbey, North Facade

Winter Evening Blues —
Westminster Bridge

Westminster Abbey –
The Great West Door

Be Proud – London 2012 Olympics

198

DECIMO·EDWARDI·SEPTIMI·REGIS·
REGINÆ·CIVES·GRATISSIMI·MDCCCC

Building To The Edge – The Thames

Do You Have A Dream,
No Not Yet — The Shard

Retro & Modern Architecture – Willis & Lloyds Buildings

Gherkin Stripes

203

The Kew Pagoda

St Pancras Railway Station & Hotel, Euston Road

I Was The Tallest — One Canada Square Canary Wharf

206

Three of the many Thames Dockside Cranes

207

Out Of My Comfort Zone – Walking Into Selfridges

The Gherkin – 30 St Mary Axe

Night On The Town – Trafalgar Square London City

The Sphinx (One of the pair from Cleopatra's Needle) – Victoria Embankement

Harrod's Department Store, Brompton Road Knightsbridge

213

Harrod's Department Store, Brompton Road Knightsbridge

Natural History Museum – South Kensington

MI6 Building SIS Headquarters —Vauxhall Cross

New Scotland Yard – Metropolitan Police Service

217

The Cenotaph War Memorial – Whitehall

The Dorchester Hotel – Park Lane

Duck Tours - The Amphibious Tour Buses

Boadicea (Boudica) and Her Daughters – Westminster London

First published in 2015 by New Holland Publishers Pty Ltd
London • Sydney • Auckland

The Chandlery Unit 009 50 Westminster Bridge Road London SE1 7QY United Kingdom
1/66 Gibbes Street Chatswood NSW 2067 Australia
5/39 Woodside Ave Northcote, Auckland 0627 New Zealand

www.newhollandpublishers.com

ISBN 9781742577517

Managing Director: Fiona Schultz
Publisher: Alan Whiticker
Project Editor: Jessica McNamara
Designer: Peter Guo
Production Director: Olga Dementiev
Printer: Toppan Leefung Printing Limited

10 9 8 7 6 5 4 3 2 1

Keep up with New Holland Publishers on Facebook
www.facebook.com/NewHollandPublishers

Simon Hadleigh-Sparks is an award winning London based amateur photographer that draws his inspiration form the city around him. Completely self taught Simon discovered his passion for photography quite late in life. His eye for clean lines, architectural design and subtle incorporation of human elements inspires him to create unique, original and often thought-provoking images. Completely self taught and still learning, Simon's ambition is to continue his work, experimenting with extreme contrast and earning himself the title of 'Master of Light'. Using a mixture of styles of photography, including reflected imagery Simon is embracing a new photographic perspective of urban landscapes.

His photographs are his stories and he is now at a point in his life where he can express himself through this medium. His recent successes include winner and best in show at the 2014 London Photo Festival, highly commended in the 2014 Urban Photographer of the Year and 3rd place in the monochrome category of the 2014 International Garden Photographer of the Year, as well as being acknowledged in 2014 as one of '8 Street Photographers that Rock Our World' on the popular blog, Lightstalking.

Simon is a professional gardener in Syon Park, West London, a husband and a father. His photography is a hobby, a passion that he shares in the hope of inspiring others along the way.